More Graded Stuc
for Clarinet

Book Two

Clarinet study repertoire with supporting Simultaneous Learning elements

Edited and selected by Paul Harris

FABER *ff* MUSIC

©2015 by Faber Music Ltd
Bloomsbury House
74-77 Great Russell Street
London
WC1B 3DA

Music setting by MusicSet2000
Cover design by Chloë Alexander
Page design by Susan Clarke

Printed in England by Caligraving Ltd

ISBN10: 0-571-53927-0
EAN13: 978-0-571-53927-7

To buy Faber Music publications or to find out about the full range of titles available
please contact your local music retailer or Faber Music sales enquiries:
Faber Music Ltd, Burnt Mill, Elizabeth Way, Harlow CM20 2HX
Tel: +44 (0) 1279 82 89 82   Fax: 44 (0) 1279 82 89 83
sales@fabermusic.com   fabermusicstore.com

Introduction

This sequel to *80 Graded Studies* presents a rich and exciting diversity of music designed to explore all manner of technical and musical ingredients. The two books comprising this collection offer study material for clarinet players, arranged progressively from elementary level to Grade 8. They have been carefully chosen to represent all styles of music, from the traditional classical and romantic repertoire to jazz and other contemporary national styles, and to explore all basic techniques necessary for the developing player.

The collection has been devised very much with the Simultaneous Learning approach in mind. Each study has been given four ingredients for the player to explore, plus one empty bubble in which to add the key (or keys). The intention is that the student will begin work on a study by examining that key – through its scale, arpeggio and any other related patterns – and then by making connections and experimenting with the other four ingredients – all done before actually playing from bar 1. In this way each study will generate an interesting and engaging 'project' to help players focus on and develop the core technical and musical challenges presented, rather than simply being another piece to learn.

I would like to thank Jean Cockburn for all her considerable help in putting these volumes together; also Jonathan Howse, Julia Middleton and Lesley Rutherford. Especial thanks to Mary Chandler, whose superb editing and imagination have helped create a really engaging study collection for the twenty-first century clarinet player.

Paul Harris, 2015

52

articulation colour · crossing registers · syncopation · wide leaps · Key ____

Zazz

Fast (straight 8s) (♩ = 132)

Paul Harris

53

pp *staccato* | **lyrical phrasing** | **rhythmic freedom** | **sustaining airflow** | **Key** _____

Andante (♩. = 50)

Frédéric Berr

54

accents and *fz*   descending leaps   energetic rhythms   grace notes   Key _____

Gypsy air

Carl Baermann

Allegretto molto moderato (♩ = 60)

© 2015 by Faber Music Ltd

55

cadenzas   elegant triplets   extended *cresc.* and *dim.*   high-register *staccato*   Key _____

Theme and variation

Ernesto Cavallini

9

57

⁵⁄₄ time   contrasts in style   smooth *legato*   weight of ornaments   Key _____

Lament and dance

Lento espressivo (♩ = 60)

László Nitski

© 2015 by Faber Music Ltd

10

58

character changes · clean fingerwork · crisp rhythms · dynamic changes · Key _____

Allegro giusto (♩ = 92)

Hermann Lange

2nd time to Coda ⊕

⊕ **Coda**

59

controlled leaps · hairpins · precise finger movement · varying tone colour · Key _____

Hyacinthe Klosé

60

jumps between registers

economical finger movement

precise articulation

sustaining repeated patterns

Key _____

Allegro brilliante (♩ = 160)

Franz Thaddäus Blatt

© 2015 by Faber Music Ltd

62

Allegro con moto (♪ = 200)

Søren Silkeborg

63

accents and *sf*

energetic character

even *staccato*

stamina

Key
_____

Allegro vivo (♩. = 108)

Franz Thaddäus Blatt

embouchure control

maintaining motor rhythms

tone quality above D3

wide leaps

Key _____

Theme and variation

Maestoso (♩ = 50)

Ernesto Cavallini

Variation (♩ = 60)

65

economic finger movement   ornate playing   subdividing beats   sustaining tone   Key _____

Adagio (♩ = 60)

Heinrich Baermann

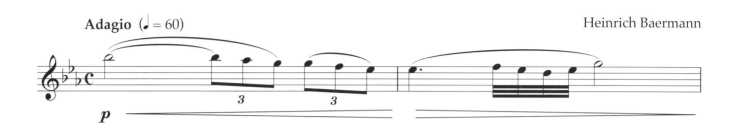

66 alternative fingerings · even tone in leaps · intonation · *legato* in busy key-work · Key _____

Moderato (♩ = 50)

Ludwig Wiedemann

67

breath support · light fingers · quick character changes · witty style · Key _____

Introduction, theme and variations microscopicoso

Freely, with a feeling of virtuoso

Paul Harris

Variation 4: Relaxing on some green 'grassioso'

Variation 5: 'Humoroso'

pp (cheekily)

Variation 6: Furioso

Finale – tempo 'comodioso'

68

fp   precise articulation   two-in-a-bar   vivid dynamics   Key

Ludwig Wiedemann

   © 2015 by Faber Music Ltd

69

Poco allegro (♩ = 88)

Hyacinthe Klosé

© 2015 by Faber Music Ltd

70 delicate articulation finger precision high-register slurring short, resonant *staccato* Key _____

Grade 7

Marionettes

Vif (♪. = 112)

Jean-Luc Dessein

71

alternative fingerings · reading unusual sharps · sustaining melodic lines · throat note tone · Key _____

Andante (♩. = 50)

Cyrille Rose

© 2015 by Faber Music Ltd

72

capricious style · freedom of tempo · note lengths · short-note resonance · Key

Fantasy
for Mark Walton

Paul Harris

73

break crossings

grace-note precision

two-register slurred leaps

Key
_____

Andante (♩. = 80)

Hyacinthe Klosé

74

character shifts | expressive *staccato* | flexible embouchure | sustaining a beautiful tone | Key _____

Variations sentimentales

Carl Baermann

Grade 8 ✓

75

expressive virtuosic style | even air column | light *staccato* (all dynamics) | relaxed fingers | Key
_____

Ernesto Cavallini

Adagio (♩ = 50)

76

brilliancy of performance   clean fingerwork   focusing tone quality   mixed articulation   Key _____

Andante sostenuto (♩ = 80)

Aurelio Magnani

77

attack on accents changing time signatures clarity on note repetition precise articulation Key _____

Furiant

Allegro furioso (♪ = ♪ throughout = 208)

István Kleiper

78

dynamic contrasts · economic finger movement · even semiquavers · tune and accompaniment · Key _____

Hyacinthe Klosé

ff staccato

confident
support

agile finger
movement

extending
altissimo
range

Key
_____

Ludwig Weidemann

Allegretto e cantabile (♩ = 88)

© 2015 by Faber Music Ltd

80

altissimo register fingering

exciting dotted rhythms

flamboyant style

warm tone in upper register

Key

_____

Grade 8

Henry Lazarus

Allegro moderato ($\quad$ = 70)

© 2015 by Faber Music Ltd